Now I am sitting in the middle of my empty room
as in an aquarium
and talking with ghosts of the fishes
I used to recognize by words,
talking with the shadows floating
over the flyers ripped off street poles.

"I love my accent...
I love my accent..."
I repeat and repeat again
just not to ask myself:

Who am I now.
Am I real or just the black fish
my grandfather failed to catch.

Immigrant Blues

Sorry, Mother, sorry
I didn't have the heart to tell you I died that day
when I reached the border.
Customs officials could tell you about that
if they still remember the boy
with a burning suitcase in one hand
and an empty extinguisher in another.
They took everything from me,
even the flag I was wrapped in when I was born.
I could keep just what wasn't written in my
Customs Declaration:
just sorrow, memory and pain.
It's hard to live as a mouse
once you've died as the cat.

I am lonely, Mother,
lonely as a forgotten toy in the window of a shop shut for
                                                    Christmas,
lonely as the strange face in my mirror.
Only the neighbour's cat notices how gently
I am locking up the door behind me
going to the bar to smile
and how hard I slam it
when I come back.

The postman thinks I am weird for paying
so much for parcels to be sent
to an unknown address
just to be returned at my birthday.
But he's just a postman
and he doesn't know much about the beautiful smell
of trains and distant countries
that the cardboard spreads for months.

He doesn't know much about
how wind caught in his raincoat reminds me
of the wind on our burning house that day
when I left.
I can still feel smoke in the air.

But Mother,
the chunk of our homeland's soil I smuggled
turned into a dust
no different from the dust on the streets
I walk every day searching for a shortcut back.
The sorrow sometimes has the shape of beauty
when the leaves start falling in the same way
they do in my memory.

Even the skin of my apartment walls became
smooth and friendly
letting me hear my neighbour crying
at the radio news from a country I never heard of.
Does he listen to me while I loudly read the letter
I sent to myself?
I don't know.
But it's a pleasant feeling not being the only mouse
in the country of cats.

An Immigrant Poem

for Aleksandar Bukvić

We who doze in sleepy subways at dawn
and read yesterday's newspapers in city buses
have never missed our Saturday evenings.
We meet in a bar and talk about the homeland.

We swallow beer greedily as if washing down the sickness
that inhabits our stomach every Monday
with the alarm-clock ringing
and the anxious face of an employer who doesn't understand
the point of talking about homeland and politics.

There, springs smell of childhood,
there, mother smells of kitchen towels,
there, people have time to love.

We gaze at each other like conspirators
and speak in low voices.
We whisper to prevent some smart-ass
at the table next to us asking:
Why don't you go back to your homeland
when you suffer so much here
and everything is better there.
We would then have to justify ourselves
with unpaid loans
and children who don't want to go back,
only to drive away a terrible doubt
that obsesses us like a disease,
doubt that perhaps
those for whom we would return
don't live in the homeland anymore.

There, birds sing more beautifully,
there, passion perfumes the air,
there, men sit in bars even on Mondays.

We drink and talk politics
and each of our words is as precise
as the bill that arrives after the drinks.
We whisper to prevent the waitress from saying
that we could have already returned to the homeland rich
if only we had avoided the Saturday evenings
for all these years.

What do waiters know about nostalgia?
What does the homeland know about our sorrow?
What do Saturdays know about our Mondays?

We drink and talk
as if curing ourselves of a fatal illness one dies from
only on Saturdays.
We talk to prevent someone's mentioning
that a hangover's as ugly
in the homeland
as here.

Sacrifice

I saw Carol again. I hardly recognized her.
She didn't recognize me at all.
She does not resemble her photograph anymore
from page 326
of the *Oxford Archeological Encyclopedia.*

I found her pinning the photograph
of a missing two-year-old boy
to the bulletin board in a skyscraper
and begging for any information.

Thirty years ago
when her passion for discovery ignited,
she left her son in the care of a friend
and went to dig in the hot Egyptian soil
looking for history in bones.

Two years later she returned with the discovery
that the ancient Egyptians, in honour of God,
sacrificed a few boys every year.
All the newspapers wrote about that
and her fame grew taller
than all the sacrificed boys.

But somebody else was living in her friend's apartment
who knew nothing about the boy or the previous tenant.
Her friend had disappeared
and the policemen just shrugged their shoulders
whenever she took out the boy's picture
from the wallet still full of Egyptian sand.

I saw Carol again.
She does not resemble at all the photograph of the Carol
who discovered the terrible truth about
sacrificing boys thousands of years ago.

Wherever they invite her to give a lecture
on that shameful history of sacrifice,
she carries copies of her missing son's picture
and leaves them in the cities
whose names she can't even remember.
She does that at night when shame is not visible.
Canada is big, I told her in passing.
Pain is bigger than Canada and Egypt together
she told me and stared at me for a long time
as if trying to recognize in me
the face of a
two-year-old.

Kole's Cat

I heard Kole's cat think.
I could swear I did.
It was a day after the burial when a few of us
entered his rented basement room
to take what our friend left behind
to a pawn-shop.
The cat was sitting beside the empty food dish
and looking me straight in the eyes:

Look, they are packing up books on which
I lay longer than Kole spent reading them.
I can easily remember each page on which
he would start crying
and I would sit on his lap and console him.

They are taking away the couch
on which Kole would fall asleep fully dressed
and I would climb on his chest and warm
the cold constellation of wine stains on his shirt.

They are packing up even the blanket
that still smells of my kittens.
I never managed to teach them
not to eat leftovers from Kole's plate.
Then the kittens left and I stayed to play with spiders
and guard the sacred silence
of our small basement apartment.

They are taking away the piano I would lie on
while Kole played sad songs
that none of them has ever heard.
I know every one by heart.
They are stored in my stomach
just like Kole's terrible cough when he returned
late at night in his dirty work clothes.
Those coarse hands hadn't caressed anyone
so tenderly as they caressed me.

They are taking away everything.
But nobody has touched my food dish,
the smallest thing in this room,
as if they are all afraid
of live memories
stored in me.

If

If on the subway my hand accidentally touched yours
on that merciless ride every evening back
to my cold bachelor apartment
perhaps you would look for my shy eyes
hidden under the cap
and think:
Is this the man who empties a pocket of silence into my
voice mail
a few times every day?

In the crowded train
nobody would notice me caressing a strand of your hair
that insolently smells of my pillow.
Nobody but you.
Perhaps for a moment you would think
that the world is full of lonely people
including the one
who has been sending unsigned Christmas cards
for years.

If I leaned on you tenderly
in that packed train full of tired or sleepy people
perhaps you would feel the fire in my skin
and wish to warm yourself one stop longer
on the shoulder of the shy weirdo
whose warmth reminds you of something
you have forgotten,
thinking:
The world is full of cold people with north in their bosoms
who fear touch might melt their ice.

I could have touched your hand if you hadn't got off
at the stop where you never get off.
I only needed a moment to show you
your earring
alive in my pocket all these years.
The same one I found in my bed
so long ago
before you forgot me.

But who knows if you would recognize it at all?
You would think:
The world is full of lonely people
and lost earrings.

Hasan's Case

(Reza's story)

One night
when heat made the air stink of decay
in the refugee camp
taciturn Hasan told us how he survived the firing squad in Iran.
They arrested him one day when
he told his co-workers during lunchbreak in the silver mine
that he had seen God in a dream
gripping a canister of gasoline in one hand
and a piece of hashish in the other.
He didn't know that there was a revolution going on
and that God had authorized the Police
to deal with dreams.

They blindfolded him, took him to the courtroom
and sentenced him along with thousands of others.
He didn't even hear his own sentence
over the moans and cries.
Sandals were put on his feet
and he shuffled for a long time in the dark line
before he asked someone behind him
where they were going.

To be killed, replied the man
as if they were going for a picnic.
Those who are sentenced to exile get leather sandals
he explained,
the rest of us get cardboard ones
lasting until we reach the firing squad.
Your sandals creak like leather.

Hasan said he lay on the ground and howled
until the last prisoner stepped over him
and then they rewarded him with exile.

God had his fingers there, commented a history professor.
Sheer luck, said a former priest.
Curiosity saved him, added a gambler.
Why do you talk so much, murmured a sleepy politician.

Who knows how long we would have argued
but it was already morning
and a nurse came to bandage Hasan's bruised back.
After that we went silent.
We all pretended that we were sleeping
and that we couldn't hear Hasan's moaning
as if he were being stepped on by people
dead or alive.

Not one of us knew which they were
because we couldn't tell the difference between
the creaking of leather
and cardboard sandals.

A Report on a Boy and an Encyclopedia

During the three-year siege of my city
when images of burned houses, killed people
and columns of refugees
were on TV news across the world
a twelve-year-old boy in Italy committed suicide.
The short note he left said
that he couldn't bear the scenes of bloody war anymore.

Poor boy.
I can imagine the nervous pencil in his hand
fighting with the page
torn from his school notebook.
I can see the moment
when the open window of the attic apartment
seemed closer to him than the cold TV screen.

His death lasted briefly in the media.
It lasted as long as the discussions on
how advisable it was to show images
of our imperfect world to carefree citizens.

Somehow, at the same time, in the same country,
a new edition of the *European Encyclopedia* came out
in which there wasn't a single word under the letter B
about the terrible war going on in Bosnia.
There were pictures of bridges that had been destroyed,
museums that had disappeared in flame,
and tourists were invited to visit the sights
that had been turned into minefields.

I can imagine the calm hand of the author on the keyboard
copying information about the dying country
from some long-dead book.
Behind him is a TV set
dusty and out of order for years.

For days I tried to find a connection among
the boy, the writer and myself
who had been hurt in some strange way.
I didn't find anything
except that
the boy's death denied the writer
and the writer denied the death of the boy.
I was not there at all.

I'm afraid that
one day, tired of wars and books,
I'll come across the *European Encyclopedia*
and ask myself:
What is this newspaper clipping doing
in the pages under the letter B.
The boy's sad face might end up in the garbage,
the book might continue to live on the shelf
and I
staring at the TV news
might not notice that I became
the only victim.

The Book of Rebellion

Nobody anymore remembers the secret book
that nobody ever dared mention.
Not even I who think that wisdom comes with age.
It was passed on secretly from hand to hand
like a forbidden legend that was only guessed,
and bound people with the sweet glue of curiosity
and heavy chains of caution and fear.

I took it over in the basement of the old maternity hospital
that they turned into a prison.
A man shoved it into my hands
warning me to forget his face that very instant
and making me swear that the book
would never get into the hands of the police.
I didn't even manage to tell him
how proud I was at joining.
He disappeared the same way
I disappeared the following week
after handing over the book to somebody else.
Those years of waiting for changes seemed harder than
waiting in lines for food, pencils and paper.

Now that I think about it,
I never learned the name of the book
nor were its contents ever clear to me.
Its sentences were so soaked
in the tears and sweat of former readers
that I could only make out every third word,
words like: homeland, Rebellion, destruction and future.
And the title page with the author's name
had been erased by sweaty fingers
before it reached me.

Today,
when lines in front of public libraries
seem longer and longer,
it occurs to me that all of us
thousands of readers
were somehow the authors of that book.

But, the same President still rules the homeland.
He grew old in power the same way
we grow old in waiting.
During statutory holidays everybody notices
the smile hovering on his face
when in his celebratory speech
he mentions the mythical Book of Rebellion
supposedly devised by
troublemakers and manipulators.

Just like the smile of somebody who
a long time ago
made a good joke
that is still being retold.

Bill's Uniform

Bill has got a new uniform.
Buttons shine like medals,
the collar is sharp as a sword,
and he can't hide the pleasure of
watching his figure
reflected in a prisoner's eyes.
Even the ugly immigrants behind the bars
look less dangerous today.

Don't show them a human face, you are an angel
and your uniform is protected land.
And don't forget:
The more you despise them,
the more they respect you
as his father once told him
just before being retired to the police graveyard.

Politics sometimes change
but police uniforms are always the same
because we are all guilty
in one way or another,
thinks Bill
while walking along the cells
and turning off the lights.

Tonight, Bill will walk his uniform
along the main street making prostitutes cheer up,
then have juice in his father's favourite pub
where stinking drunks look suspicious
and the barman's skin seems too dark.
Then he will turn on the alarm of his clock,
watching the street lights
shining on the buttons.

Goodnight, father, he will say to the picture on the wall.
Goodnight, boy, the neighbour next door will say.

But now,
still turning off lights in the prison corridor,
in the last cell he notices a pair of eyes
watching him, so sharp
that he feels naked
walking over felt buttons like dying stars.
The pair of eyes reminds him of
his mother's sharp eyes,
sharp as his collar, long ago,
when he was driven home by a police car
after he had beaten up a newcomer,
some ugly schoolmate
in a wheelchair.

On the Bike

I am riding my bike. The pedals are already hot.
The odometer says I am far from a sudden heart attack
and every drop of my sweat says I am closer
to my bored young wife who has just arrived
and who sometimes cries for no reason.
I can do better. I can ride faster.

Is it Wojcek, that guy sitting in front of the funeral home?
Once a famous disc jockey back home,
he sold a great record collection to buy a ticket
to the promised land.
Now he's listening to painful silence
broken only by coins jingling in his hat.

I can do better. I can ride faster.

No, it couldn't be Vesna walking along the stripbar street
in a skirt that hides nothing.
She came on the same flight I did
to get married to someone she met through a pen-pal exchange.
I guess it's the same tattooed bastard
who is shouting from his car at her
to unbutton her blouse and smile.
Does he know she was once a ballerina?

I can do better. I can ride faster.

That grey man crossing the street in a wheelchair,
I hope it's not Jan.
Once a photographer, now just a frame.
Obsessed with lotteries, he served for years as a lab rat
renting his body for military experiments.
The day he won big money

he came down with a rotting illness
no one had heard of before.
Now he spends his money buying deodorants
to quell the stench on his way to the casino.

I can do better. I can ride faster.

It's OK for today,
my trainer tells me,
get off the stationary bicycle
and don't bother asking for more time.
There are lots of newcomers waiting for you to stop.
Take your fear and your ghosts with you
on the way to the shower
and see you next week.

You can do it better. You can ride faster.

Literature Professor at the Funeral

I once knew an ugly poet who wrote such beautiful poems
that every couple learned them by heart
as a pass to the world of love.
He was so ugly that some couples would tear posters
announcing his readings off the walls.
We had a cruel joke that he'd get a woman
if he wore a gas mask.

That summer,
when roses refused to blossom
because of gunpowder inhabiting the air,
some time after midnight on the road to the city,
he picked up a strange hitchhiker
who entertained him from the back seat
reciting his poetry without knowing who he was.
After travelling with this stranger for an hour
he fell in love with her,
and in the second hour of the drive he proposed to the voice
whose owner he couldn't recognize in the rearward dark.
How he must have burned with curiosity
when at the first stop in front of the mountain washroom
he flicked the lighter to see the beauty
and his hands started shaking.

She went to the washroom and disappeared.
He never saw her again.
He spent all night in the stinky mountain washroom
reciting his most beautiful love poems.

You know, he told me once, before he died,
I've lost her only because of my curiosity.
Not because of that, I thought,

when you flicked the lighter to see her
you should have known she would see you too.
How much of your pain must have remained in her.

At his funeral I met an ugly woman
who was whispering his poems in the second row.
I called out to her that I knew the reason
why all publishers refused to print
his photograph on his books.

You don't know anything about poetry,
she told me
and went to the end of the row,
far from my students
who were entertaining themselves
by kicking an empty lighter
on the street.

This year
again the roses have refused to blossom.
Some say it is because of gunpowder
that inhabits the air.
Who knows?

The War Is Over, My Love

The war is over. I guess.
At least that's what the morning paper says.
On the front page there is a picture of the factory
that until yesterday produced only flags.
It is starting to make pyjamas today.

On the next page there is a report on the posthumous
awarding of medals and then there are crossword puzzles
and national lottery results
in which they regret to inform that this month
again nobody won the grand prize.

Pharmacies work all night again,
radio plays the good old hits
and it seems as if there never was a war.

I enter an old clothing shop
and on the hangers I recognize my neighbours:
There,
Ivan's coat. We used the lining for bandages.
Look,
Hasan's shoes. Shoelaces are missing.
And Jovan's pants. The belt is gone.

But where are the people?
I run along the main street
to look at myself in the shop windows
but the shop windows are smashed
and there are only naked mannequins
that will wear new pyjamas tomorrow
according to the morning paper.

Then I run into our apartment
and look at myself in the glass
on your picture on the wall
and I don't care if I am not the same anymore,
the one who cried when they were taking you away.

You told me you would come back
my love
when the war is finally over.

The war is over.
At least according
to the morning paper.

A Scene, after the War

for Luna and Darije

I'd never been aware how beautiful my house is
until I saw it burning,
my schoolmate told me, who had twenty pieces of shrapnel
that remained deep under his skin after the war.
He wrote me how at the airport he enjoyed
having upset the customs officials who couldn't understand
why the checkpoint metal detector howled for no reason.

I had never been aware I was a nation
until they said they'd kill me,
my friend told me,
who'd escaped from a prison camp
only to be caught and raped by Gypsies
while she was roaming in the woods.
Then they sold her to some Italian pimps
who tattooed the owner's brand and number on her fist.
She says you cannot see it when she wears gloves.

I recognized them in a small town in Belgium.
They were sitting and watching the river
carry plastic bags, cans,
and garbage from the big city.
She was caressing the hard shrapnel lumps
through his shirt
and he was caressing her glove.

I wanted to say hello
and give them a jolly photograph from the times
when none of us knew the meaning
of House and Nation.

Then I realized that there was more meaning
in the language of silence
in which they were seeing off
the plastic bags down the river
than in the language
in which I would have tried to feign those faces
from the old photograph
that shows us all smiling long ago.

At the End of the Century

In my opinion
the twentieth century didn't last long,
perhaps just a few years,
enough for me to learn to walk
and to pretend that falls didn't hurt.
That's when I also learned that
it was best to wrap wounds
in bandages made of one's skin.

I am a boy who was sitting alone for too long
in an empty classroom waiting for the teacher
who never came.
The only reminder of him was the chalk on his desk
and I kept standing in front of the empty blackboard
to daydream,
locked in the empty school.

Hidden behind the curtain,
I learned everything I learned
by peeking through the window.
I grieved for every death,
I was happy about every birth
and I commiserated with street revolutionaries
when they dispersed with torn banners.

The twentieth century didn't last long,
perhaps just enough for me to learn
how silence could purr beautifully
and how loneliness bites terribly.

I didn't have time to fall in love
with the pair of hands that pasted
the demolition order for the school,
with the wet eyes of the policewoman who took me away,
with the angelic face of the female doctor
in the retirement home.

The beloved woman I've never met
lulls my children to sleep.

I haven't managed to grow old in such a way
that at least the pigeons in the park notice when I'm gone.
I happened to grow old inside,
like a watermelon
that dreamed of August for too long
and woke up into a December morning.

All I have taken from life is the chalk
the teacher left behind
that seems to me as big as the universe
while I look at it through the eyes
of a boy who has only started to learn.

On Graveyards and Flowers

When I was twelve
on statutory holidays
I would secretly go to the Graveyard of Heroes at night
and steal fresh carnations from wreaths.
I would wrap them in cellophane
and sell them in the evenings
to enamoured couples in restaurants.
With the money I earned I would buy books.
At the time I thought that I would find a solution in books
to the mysterious relation between
wars and carnations.

In the meantime there were so many wars
that the graveyard spread almost
to the doors of the maternity hospital.
Nobody sells carnations in restaurants anymore
because there are fewer boys and more heroes.
Besides, fresh carnations in wreaths
have been replaced by plastic roses
because nobody has time anymore
to deal with flowers.

Now when I am almost fifty
I sometimes have the impression that
I haven't moved far from that twelve-year-old boy.
Only now
I sell my audience
those same old graves
for a few flowers on stage
beside the glass of water
and the microphone.

HANGOVERS

Father and Bees

for Vesa Toijonen

Now I know that my father hasn't learned anything about war.
He hasn't learned anything about bees, either.
At the beginning of World War II
he put on a uniform and went to fight against Fascism
leaving the family home and his beehives.
When the bees went wild and started attacking children,
the locals suffocated them with smoke.
After two years of the new war,
he went to the old family house
and started raising bees again.
He stopped reading newspapers,
he swears at the authorities less and less
and disappears when someone starts talking
about politics.

He sent me a jar of honey. I haven't opened it yet.

I've heard that some 10 kilometers from the old family house
4,000 people were killed and buried.
I've heard that the stench of rotting corpses
buried at the soccer field overpowers the smell of linden.
They say that nobody can sleep at night
from the detonations of the empty stomachs of the dead
that explode in the summer heat.

My father doesn't know that.
He only raises bees and sends jars of honey.

I skim through the encyclopedias to find out
how far bees can fly and do they run away from stench.
Then I start crying.
And I can't explain to my children why I forbid them

to open the jar of honey that my father sent them.
The warrior and beekeeper
who has never learned anything about the war
or about the bees.

A Thick Red Line

for Fraser Sutherland

A lamb escaped from me
and I sent the wolf to bring it back.
Many such lambs loiter about the forest,
and leave droppings where I like to watch the valley.

I am afraid something might happen to the wolf.
There are many fugitive lambs
and very few such faithful wolves.
Years pass before you train them
not to look you in the eyes
but at your hands.

I've read in an encyclopedia
how many people were killed in Auschwitz.
Like lambs.
Later I read a book about the same camp
but 308 victims were missing from the list.

Between those two books
my wolf treads in the deep snow
and draws a thick red line with his tail,
contentedly sniffing the air.
The spring is coming again
when the snow melts as fast as memory
and lambs feel the urge to escape.

A Note on the Forest and You

I followed you to the first tree
that spring when we were so poor
and at home we banned the words
calendar and clock.
I followed your lean shadow which ingratiated itself
to the invisible border behind which
the forest began,
cold as a military formation.

Look,
on a 100-year-old beech a sailor engraved
his rank and the name of his darling.
What is their love like now
and does the name still compare to the rank?

In the bark of an oak, bullets glitter
like a constellation by somebody learning
how to handle a gun.
Whose face did he imagine while aiming?
Did his finger sweat while reaching for the cold trigger
where the beauty of persuasion
was turning into noise?

Even that fallen tree
resembles the tree behind our house
in which my grandfather used to hide his gun
and I pretended not to see.
Until both my grandfather and the gun disappeared.

I followed you to the first tree
that spring when poverty seemed to you
as visible as a uniform.
Then the forest surrounded you
and your voice turned into a shot.

Have you seen my grandfather
who is wandering through the forest
with an army of shadows
perfectly unaware of the meaning of calendar and clock?
Is the ghost of a sailor
now engraving your name into a tree?
I am trying to unravel this
in the constellation of bullets
in the bark of the oak
behind which begins the world
where I don't know how to belong.

I Haven't Learned Anything

I was engaged in studying forests and reading roots
and pretended I didn't see anything else than
what went unnoticed by the others.
I knew the history of every tree,
the origin of moss,
the age of every squirrel
and I didn't even notice when the city police
changed their uniforms.

In town there were already hordes of quacks
offering recipes for eternal life in exchange for food.

Doctors were leaving hospitals and appearing on TV screens
offering the poor get-rich-quick solutions.

Incorruptible judges were going out to drink
with those they once sentenced.

Women were walking with dark circles under their eyes
and forgetting to pick up their children from day care.

Horoscopes became the most popular literature
and books of prophets were circulated as widely
as toilet tissue.

I pretended I didn't notice that my history professor
took off his hat and greeted the worst pupils
who were walking along the main street of the city
with revolvers at their belts.

I passed by the high school in which I spent years
learning about the kindness of people
and the happy endings of wars.
Refugees live there now.

I spent years there studying the dignified language of

                                                    persuasion

and didn't learn anything.

Not even some simple words
with which I could restrain a man with an axe in his hand
measuring the maple tree
under the high school windows.
The same maple tree that for years,
by some invisible language,
persuaded me that every tree in the forest
had its name and its root and its soul.

The same maple tree
whose first leaf I glued in my herbarium
believing I was starting to learn.

In the Time of Hunger

In the time of hunger we lived on memories.
We rolled remains of tobacco in Bible paper
and put them into empty packs of Marlboros.

We made Cognac by mixing pure alcohol with tea
and poured it into empty bottles of the best Scotch.

We went to hungry markets with the bags
of the world's leading fashion companies.

While drinking our first coffee we talked about
TV serials from the past
and nobody mentioned the dead
and us who resembled them.

I remember that my Uncle Matija,
long ago, quarrelled with my father over an inheritance
so bitterly that they haven't exchanged a word for five years.
Once in the country pub he got drunk
and started cursing my father and calling him
a Communist and wastrel.
One of the local drunks,
recognizing a good chance for a free glass of brandy,
agreed with my uncle's opinion
upon which my uncle slapped him and said:
I can say the most terrible things about my brother
but I can't let you insult him.

During the war
a foreign journalist showed up in town
and after the poor dinner we offered him said
that freedom should come as soon as possible
at least to spare us
from eating slops.

Later he knocked on our door in vain,
and was surprised that we didn't want
to recognize him anymore,
on our way to the hungry market
with bags from the leading fashion companies,
while smoking stinking tobacco from Marlboro packs,
looking for something
that only we can call garbage.

Goldfish

At the time when even beggars were ashamed to beg
I traded my grandfather's gilded medals
to a soldier for a goldfish.
I put it in a big glass jar
that had held candies in better times
and gave it to my children for my birthday.

Sometimes for days we would forget to feed
that taciturn being whose silence
God rewarded with gold.
For months we wouldn't change the water
but the goldfish refused to die and end its
mystical life in an ordinary toilet bowl.
I would notice it only when the fire
from a nearby building would glow on its scales,
the only light by which we could recognize
our frightened faces at night.

One morning I saw my children
kneeling by the glass jar
and begging it to end that war in which
people disappear and never return.
Then they talked of how that jar
had once been full of candies.

I thought
that I would like the soldier
from whom I got the goldfish
now to be watching my grandfather's medals
with the same grief,
and I imagine that those gilded medals
my grandfather acquired long ago
were traded
for a goldfish.

In Sarajevo with Borges

What can I bribe you with?
I offer you the howl of a man who wandered into a minefield
following the track of a runaway sheep.
I can offer you the ear of a woman I recognized
by an earring I won one year at a fair
shooting at a yellow plastic rose.

I could give you a sleeve of my sister's wedding dress
which remained in my hand while I was trying
to pull her from under the tank.
I can show you a family photograph
in which my brother in his army uniform
looms above a boy with a pencil in his hand
and an ink stain on his forehead.
You would perhaps recognize
my family history,
the family tree from which the branches fall
that I collect as kindling.
Just because I've seen
how winter kills puppies and the deserted old.

I court you as a loser, tired of the real war
which until now happened to others and in books,
and I don't wish to compare myself to the dead.
If you start to see through the eyes of a boy
who has been learning how to smile for years,
I will also smell that yellow rose of yours
you had picked long before I was born.
Until then I offer you only
twenty-eight unhappy lines.

My Dear Jorge

I have learned the beauty of your poems
and argued with your past for so long
that it was too late when I noticed that my town
resembled an ashtray.
I went for a walk with you
and nobody recognized you.
Nobody.

Not the man whose daughter was rejected by the river
that couldn't stand so much beauty.
Not the pregnant woman who offered you her belly
in exchange for your cane.
Not the muddy soldier who at night secretly
pulls out wooden crosses in the graveyard
and changes their places
to make a new arrangement of sorrow.

My Jorge, the world looks different
when words do not agree to be the homeland of horror,
the horror that is easier
when it lasts for years than
when it lasts for hours.

That is why I don't talk about you anymore.
I conceal you like a hereditary disease.
The world looks different – I force myself
to say this phrase
like a prayer to protect me from the need
for your blindness brought to me in the form of verses.
My dear Jorge.

Grave of the Unknown Soldier

My mother left the Communist Party
when they advised her not to have children.
She knew well how to measure the weight of meaning
and the clear soldierly sound of the disingenuous word "advise".
At the time she'd been given a special honour
to lead the delegation which would lay flowers
on the Grave of the Unknown Soldier.

Then she had me.

So she never went to lay flowers
on the Grave of the Unknown Soldier.
That photograph which shows her leaving the camp
surrounded by somebody else's children
never again appeared in the special issues of newspapers
and everyone forgot that they had smiled at her long ago
when the flag seemed more fragrant to her
than babies' diapers.

I think,
if the Party medal had seemed to her heavier than her stomach,
she would probably never have given birth to me.
She would have been laying flowers
on somebody else's grave.

My mother is gone.
The one who advised her not to become a mother
is also gone.
Only I remain
who do not believe that there are people
without names
when states
and all flowers have them.

Names

My mother didn't want to remember last names.
Her address book resembled a collection of first names
with strange drawings of animals beside each number
whose meanings only she knew.
The day she became mute and decided to die
I dialled in panic numbers from her phone book
trying to find the family doctor
but those who answered were:
the postman, the hairdresser,
the butcher, all those lonely old people
who wanted to exchange a few more words.

When I buried her
I happened to notice that in the grave next to hers
a wooden cross bore my first name.

The next day I came and saw her own cross
bent toward that grave.
Mom, I told her,
this one next to you doesn't have
the same last name as you and me,
and it is high time that you start
recognizing people by their last names also.
I straightened her cross and went to the family meeting
where it was to be decided
what kind of gravestone we'd erect for her.
We parted quarrelling.
My two grandmothers almost started a fight
over the size of the letters to be engraved on the marble.

The next morning I went to Mom's grave.
The cross was bent again
towards the grave next to hers
and the letters of her last name lay on the December soil.

What are you trying to tell me,
I asked her
and sat at the edge of the grave.

It seems to me
that I'm still sitting there.

A Simple Explanation

I am a plum. And you are an apple.
For a long time we've been lying in the same basket
made of dead branches.
And together we smell nicely with a smell
we lend to each other.
Only we can tell which belongs to whom.

I have nightmares that some day I'll wake up
and only your smell will remain,
the one I bear in me.

Therefore,
when I start bothering you, please,
do not persuade the pear to turn its
spoilt back on me.
It will force me upward in the basket.
Bear in mind
that the hand that reaches for fruit
sometimes doesn't think of taste.
Wait until I shrivel
because I will shrivel with the smell
that remains after you.

Please.

When I Fall Asleep and When I Wake Up

I fall asleep in the evening
with the thought that
the worst thing that can happen to a poet
is to write about his own experience.

I leave on the desk a half-drunk glass,
an ashtray full of cigarette butts
and unpaid power bills for my neighbours to see,
who still think that writing poetry by candlelight
is rather romantic.

I wake up in the morning
and see my neighbour watering flowers
and singing a song which reminds me
of my old home.
I can smell shampoo in her hair
and through the window I can almost touch
the lace on her dress
as she bends toward the flowerpots
pretending not to see me
and not to sing for me.

Then I think that there is no reason
to travel far and look for poetry
when there it is within reach.

NIGHTMARES

Airport

We are flying. I tell you, we are flying
and I smile to you deep in the womb of the airplane.
I offer you a wallet in which you will find
only dusty tickets.
I present you with white gloves,
an axe whose blade you can use as a mirror.
You keep silent, staring at
the stewardess in the army uniform.
You are silent, silent.

Sooty angels knock on windows selling medals,
necklaces of nickel-plated stars.
Handsome devil revolutionaries
offer us flocks of tamed clouds,
old goddesses trade their former splendour
and you hide behind a newspaper.

What year is this?
Do you remember your licence plate number,
do you know the number of this flight?
We are flying, I tell you,
we sacred swine are flying,
we ordinary heroes you can meet at circus box offices.
We are flying, I tell you,
though it looks to me
we haven't even left the runway.

Passport Borders

They returned my passport.
Simply, a faceless man came to my door
and brought me my passport,
still damp from last year's snow.
Your legs, he told me,
stick out of our trousers too much
and your head thinks more about the victims
of a future war than our past and our flag.
That's what he said
and ran down the stairs while
broken teeth and seagull feathers
fell out of his pockets.
He took away even his shadow.

He returned my face
that had been sitting in the police files for years,
my smile from the time when I believed
that wisdom was as big as a travel bag.
He returned my passport
when I'd forgotten I ever had it.

Perhaps he didn't know that I often travelled at night,
that my skin was full of odours
of continents unknown to him
and my room full of things meaningful only to me:
I brought an icicle from the North,
fire from the South,
a candle from the East,
wind from the West,
and I didn't have to justify to anybody
my simple need to avoid maps and routes
already trod by those who came before me.

He returned my passport.
He brought back the borders
and changed me into a simple traveller
who will be forced to compare himself.

Perhaps that's why he returned
my passport.

An Ordinary Man

I am an ordinary man with ears of ordinary silk
and I speak only with a voice I've heard somewhere,
a voice like an echo.
I've given up blunders:
that leg of mine intact in the sky was
an ordinary crutch made of rosewood
and when I talk about flowers
my voice smells of earth
in which blind moles delve.

I've given up blunders.
I know that rifle ranges, crowded at night with sad people,
were invented only because of the law
by which they protect somebody
from my gunpowder dreams.

I admit I sometimes start to cry at night
but so do the others.
I've met many people and they all resembled me.
Some hid in the bodies already used as corpses,
the others hid in corpses in which
an attentive ear can recognize a breath.
But they all had obedient eyes. And they liked dogs.
I've entered maidens' rooms filled with snow,
I've sniffed empty bedclothes and imagined
black stockings removed from maiden legs
only for me.
But so did the others.

Sometimes from the window I notice breadcrumbs
in the hair of women I once loved.
But they are now someone else's women
and now that's somebody else's bread.

I am an ordinary man and it's clear to me:
whenever I was born I'll die young.
I die every day and I am not afraid anymore
when in passing I notice my pale face
going by the other way.
That is why I sleep slowly.

Only sometimes
I am sad and begin to cry
though I don't know why.
And I feel sorry I am crying
and sorry I don't know why.

But so do the others.

I Am Afraid I'll Change

for Berge Arabian

God, I am afraid I'll change
to become one of the faces on a family photograph
in negative. It means I'll become alien: a phonograph record,
a bottle label, a can
or simply a runway built along a river.
I'll trim my fingers, cut my hair, and start thinking
the way I never thought before,
the obvious way.
It will be late when I notice the trees
which remain the same.

What if I change without being aware of it?
In the morning the sweat dripping from town monuments
I'll call dew not knowing that it isn't.
I will smell like a clown thinking of death,
I, a wine jug broken on virginal bedclothes.
Yet I won't be like that.

I am afraid I'll change.
Not because of wallpaper I'll wear.
Not because of that.
Goodness, nobody is given to choose the world.
But because the others will remain the same.
My face will humbly stand
in the line of the uncalled for
and be their leader.
And yet be one of them.

I am afraid I'll change.
It will happen for sure and there's nothing
to be done about it.
Therefore I am afraid,
O God.

To the Dining Car

Well, let's go and have another drink.
Let's go to the dining car while time gallops under us
like water gushing in the toilet of a train.
Let's go where sweaty soldiers sleep on empty beer crates,
to the end of the world of those who rule,
those with no more questions.

Let's step into the corridor as into a holiday dawn,
serene and meek,
let's pass by the open doors of lavatories
dragging wet shreds of toilet paper on our heels.
As we pass by we'll peep into compartments:
Look, a blue spider emerges from that man's mouth,
that child's head is strangely shaped,
look, that woman cannot bend her orthopedic crutch,
see, thousands of gnats cover them, look, look,
and please don't mention the candle.
Don't mention the candle.

Let's go there.
We'll press our noses to the carriage windows
trying to guess where we are
but all we'll see will be our eyes wide open in the glass.
Like the eyes of dead fish belly-up on the water.
Where we're headed or whether we'll ever get off this train
will lessen in importance.

Well, then,
let's go to the dining car and have another drink,
there where the search for destinations ends.
Let's go to the bar

where the conductor's uniform swings,
where shadows of loose women sway,
where the door opens to and fro,
to and fro,
opens both ways.

Just So

So, I was in a madhouse and understood everything. I did.
I listened to harmonious sounds of heavenly microphones
and loudspeakers of hell,
to the rain drumming on distant suitcases
I had once left somewhere by the road.
I remember that I didn't fear anything
and was mostly afraid of that.
For months I imagined I was a skeleton
decorated with medals going
through passport control.
But even that is over and everything
becomes clearer to me.

I was in prison also and listened to them beating me. I did.
I don't remember the dates but my scars do.
Like the blue jaws of a shark pulled out of the sea
I bit the air and the barrier behind me.
Secretly I kept a small mirror.
My father's sad army raincoat would enter
through the wall at night and just sit in the corner
only to be chased away by guards in the morning.
But even that is over now and everything
becomes clearer to me.

Later I remitted. I settled accounts. I did.
I left my crutches in the forest
when the wind took my father's raincoat

somewhere to the sky.
I talked to my shadow, chatted with the river god,
and many trivial details are now behind me.

But because of these things I believe
I will not die in an armchair
with a cat in my lap
and a cane at hand
one day.
By the window.

Who's That Waking Me Up?

Prisoners walk in circles. It's morning. It's dark.
Step by step they free themselves of lifelong fear.
Because of them I wake up
frightened that I don't know yet
where the wrong side starts.
I do notice that my room gets smaller every day
and I often hear masons working in the wall.
Where is the limit of shame?
Whose bed am I lying in?
Sleep, Goran, sleep.
The night exists just to prevent you
from meeting me.

Years go by, drinkable, but full of fear.
I am more and more inclined to fall. Have I fallen already?
God sometimes knocks on my frozen window
and I don't let him in because
he has the eyes of a prisoner and always asks: Why?
As if I knew.
I just half-breathe humbly and die the other half
looking for the place where the exit door used to be.
Sleep, Goran, sleep.
Prisoners do not exist.

Where are you going, father, in your slippers?
It's morning. It's dark. Sleep!
Leave that empty revolver case,
and stop walking like prisoners walk.
We're tame people and do not ask me anything.
I often meet you in myself and you always ask: Why?
As if you didn't know what's going on in your head

when you ask me on which side
medals should be worn.

To whom have you rented your son,
I ask you quietly so that mother won't hear,
blind but ever wakeful for I know she will ask me:
What's going on outside? As if I know.
Therefore, sleep, Goran, sleep
as sheep, butterflies,
tame people sleep.

A DREAM

A Dream

You will dream that you are sleeping
and dreaming how: you will sleepily imagine
something you will not remember anymore.

When you wake up
you will find
fragments of a broken mirror in your mouth,
orthopedic crutches lying beneath your bed.
The day will crawl outside
as if nothing has happened.

Only later you will discover
the bloody pillow beneath your head.

Author's Acknowledgements

The poems in this book were translated by Amela Simić except for the poems on pages 9, 11, 16, 18, 20, 34, and 36, which were written in English by the author. Some of these poems were previously published in Dutch translation in the author's book *Alledaagse Adam* (Atlas, Amsterdam), and in English in *Peace and War*, a privately printed limited edition book by the author and Fraser Sutherland, and incorporated in a short film *I do not Dream in English* (YLE, Finland) and in a multi-media project, *A Ballad of Baggage* (4 Unlimited, Toronto).

The author owes special gratitude to Fraser Sutherland, A.F. Moritz, and Višnja Brčić for their support and service on these poems in manuscript, as well as to the Canada Council for the Arts and to Massey College.

Translator's Acknowledgments

I am indebted to all those who read the translations of these poems and offered feedback and valuable comments, most of all Rhea Tregebov and Suzanne Routh. I am infinitely grateful to all my wonderful friends, my sister and my parents for their love and support. And to my children, Luna and Darije, who keep me going.

Thanks to Paolo Dilonardo, Angela Calo Carducci and the late Domenico Dilonardo for offering a warm shelter and a lot more. Deep gratitude to Marcy, Gail, Reva and Irving Gerstein for their generosity and friendship. And to Susan Sontag for making it all possible.

About the Poet

Goran Simić was born in Bosnia in 1952 and has been living in Toronto since 1996. He has published eleven books of poetry, drama, and short fiction, including the acclaimed volume of poems in English translation, *Sprinting from the Graveyard* (Oxford University  Press, 1997). In Canada, Simić has published *Peace and War*, a limited edition volume gathering poems by himself and by Fraser Sutherland; other books of his poetry and drama have been translated into nine languages. His poems are included in anthologies of world poetry, such as *Scanning the Century* (Penguin, 2002) and *Banned Poetry* (Index, 1997). He has received major literary awards from PEN USA and four times in former Yugoslavia.

About the Translator

Amela Simić is a translator and writer who moved to Canada from Bosnia. Her translations from English (among others, works by Susan Sontag, Bernard Malamud, Sylvia Plath, Joyce Carol Oates, Joseph Heller, Saul Bellow, Michael Ondaatje, Lawrence Durrell) appeared in literary magazines of the former Yugoslavia. She translated several novels and books by contemporary philosophers. Her essays and translations of Bosnian poetry were published in *Salmagundi*, *TLS*, *The Paris Review*, *Canadian Forum*, *Meta*, BBC Radio, etc. She earns a living as an arts administrator and is currently the Executive Director of Playwrights Guild of Canada.